JIMMY FALLON

REBECCA T. KLEIN

JIMMY FALLON

REBECCA T. KLEIN

ROSEN
PUBLISHING®

New York

Published in 2016 by The Rosen Publishing Group, Inc.
29 East 21st Street, New York, NY 10010

First Edition

Library of Congress Cataloging-in-Publication Data

Klein, Rebecca.
 Jimmy Fallon / Rebecca T. Klein. -- First edition.
    pages cm. -- (The giants of comedy)
 Includes bibliographical references and index.
 ISBN 978-1-4994-6254-8 (library bound)
 1. Fallon, Jimmy--Juvenile literature. 2. Television personalities--United States--Biography--Juvenle literature. 3. Comedians--United States--Biography--Juvenle literature. I. Title.
 PN1992.4.F34K55 2016
 791.4502'8092--dc23
 [B]
                                        2015025505

Manufactured in China

CONTENTS

INTRODUCTION

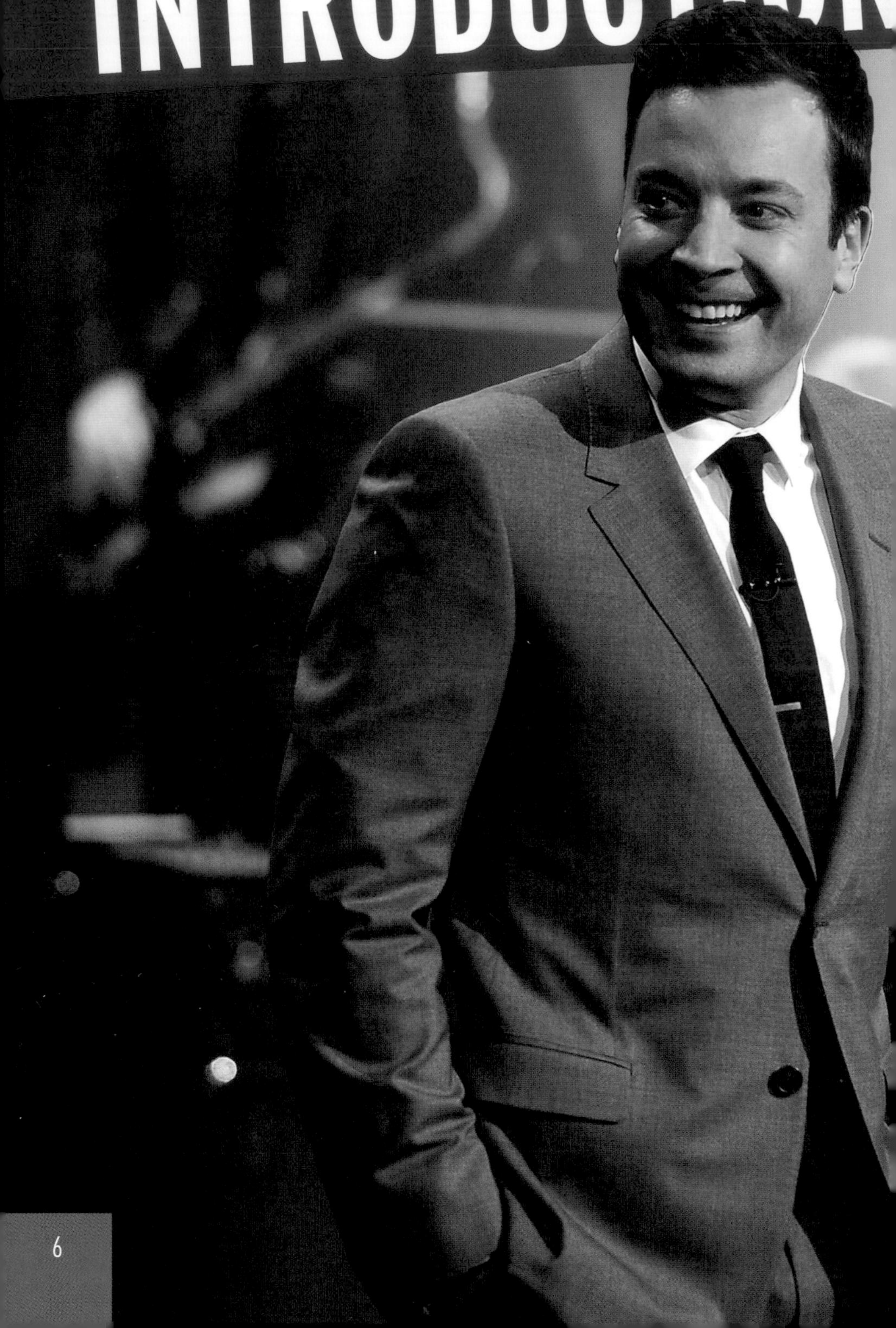

J immy Fallon's inaugural night as host of *The Tonight Show* was a declaration that he would be bringing his own flavor to the show, introducing themes and nuances that would make *The Tonight Show Starring Jimmy Fallon* unique and different from all of the previous versions of the show. Analyzing the themes introduced in this initial episode also provides a window into Jimmy Fallon's own life and into the aspects of his identity that have shaped and defined him as a comedian and as a person.

For one, Jimmy Fallon is a New Yorker. The opening vignette, directed by another prominent New York native, Spike Lee, announced that this show, like *Saturday Night Live* and *Late Night with Jimmy Fallon*, would be fully and unapologetically set in New York City, Fallon's birthplace and first home. The fact that Fallon was bringing *The Tonight Show* back to New York after many years in Los Angeles further emphasized this angle.

Fallon's joy was evident during his first episode as host of *The Tonight Show.* His welcoming smile mirrors his approachable, kind-hearted style of comedy.

Another important part of Fallon's identity stressed in the episode was that he is first and foremost a sketch comedian. No matter how many interviews he conducts and how savvy he becomes at the stand-up required for his monologue, his passion and joy is most fully evident when he is performing improv or sketch comedy and engaging in give-and-take with other comedians. This joy was on full display in the hip-hop dancing segment featuring Will Smith on the first episode of Fallon's *Tonight Show*.

The prominence of music, another important theme in Fallon's work, was evident from the very beginning of his *Tonight Show*, and the choice of musical guest for the first episode also paid homage to his Irish heritage, a strong influence in his life and his comedy. The episode included a powerful performance by prominent Irish band U2, shot on a New York City rooftop at sunset. This moment in the show beautifully and poetically tied together Fallon's love of music, New York City, and his Irish ancestry.

In addition to all of these aspects of his identity, this episode also showed audiences the personality Fallon would be bringing to the show. In his opening monologue, he said that his goal for the show was to send viewers to bed with smiles on their faces. This is, perhaps, the strongest theme in Fallon's life and the most prominent part of his identity. While some comedians use sarcasm, irony, and dark humor as their primary tools, Jimmy Fallon favors nostalgia and good-hearted humor.

This is not to say that he does not make audiences think through his comedy or that he does not critique society or engage in social commentary. However, while some comedians seem to aim to alienate themselves from audiences and interview subjects, Jimmy Fallon seems to aim for the opposite; he looks for common ground. The goal of his comedy is, very simply, to make people smile. He does this by creating an environment of inclusion in which no one is the butt of the joke and everyone is an insider.

CHAPTER ONE

Jimmy's Childhood

James Thomas Fallon Jr. was a child of New York City from the start, beginning with his birth in Bay Ridge, Brooklyn, on September 19, 1974. His parents, James Sr. and Gloria, named both of their children after themselves; Jimmy's older sister's name is Gloria, after their mother. Jimmy inherited some of his musical talent from his father, who spent his teenage years singing in various doo-wop groups in Sunset Park and Bay Ridge, with names like the Twilights and the Mellowdowns.

The family lived in Brooklyn until Jimmy was about two years old, when his father, who had by then abandoned doo-wop and gone to work for the IBM computer company, got a job in the upstate New York town of Kingston. The family moved to nearby Saugerties not only because of

Jimmy's father's new job, but also because Jimmy's parents wanted to raise their children in a quieter, cleaner environment than they could find in the five New York City boroughs in the 1970s and 1980s. Fallon talked about this move in an interview in *Jane* magazine, saying, "My parents wanted to give us a safe upbringing, a better life...for me and my sister."

Saugerties provided an idyllic setting for Jimmy's adolescent years. It wasn't until Jimmy's early adulthood, when his career began to take off, that New York City would become his home again and provide the setting for almost all of his major successes. Jimmy's childhood and adolescence in Saugerties played an extremely important role in preparing him for his career.

Jimmy and Gloria Fallon were very close during their childhood, partly because they are only a year apart in age and partly because their parents sheltered them and made them spend most of their time at home together. If they had grown up in their urban birthplace in Brooklyn, they might have spent more time exploring their wider surroundings. Instead, their backyard and living room provided the setting for most of their childhood antics. In Gloria's blog, *Growing Up Fallon*, she wrote that she and Jimmy spent most of their time in the backyard playing sports—not because they were particularly crazy about either sports or the backyard, but

Jimmy and Gloria Fallon pose with the book they cowrote. The siblings have been very close ever since their sheltered childhood in upstate New York.

because they were not allowed to do much of anything else.

Jimmy told *Spin* magazine that when he and Gloria received bikes for Christmas, they had to ride them in the backyard because they weren't allowed to ride in the street. On a different Christmas, their father bought them a basketball hoop but insisted on setting it up on the lawn. "You can't dribble on grass!" joked Jimmy. "People would walk by and think 'Those weird little Fallon kids, why don't they leave their lawn. They're the Lawn Kids!'"

The Living Room Stage

While Jimmy and Gloria were sometimes embarrassed by their parents' overprotective nature and sometimes felt stifled by all of the time they were required to spend at home together, there were definitely some benefits to this type of upbringing that would pay off later in Jimmy's career. For one thing, all of the time he spent indoors resulted in voracious consumption of television and pop culture and gave him plenty of time to study everything he was viewing and listening to. While the backyard gave Jimmy and Gloria a place to play sports, their house provided a stage for them to experiment with comedy, music, and acting. Jimmy learned to play guitar when he was thirteen, and by that time the siblings, especially Jimmy, were big fans of *Saturday Night Live.*

Dan Aykroyd and Steve Martin play "two wild and crazy guys" in one of their signature *SNL* sketches. Jimmy Fallon imitated this and other sketches as a child watching at home.

Their parents did not let them watch the live broadcasts; instead, they would tape episodes on the VCR for the kids to watch later, censoring any sketches they found to be vulgar or too adult. Jimmy and Gloria often reenacted the sketches they saw on the tapes, performing them for their parents in the living room. They dressed up in their parents' 1970s' clothes and performed as the popular characters of the era, like Dan Aykroyd and Steve Martin's Two Wild and Crazy Guys, sometimes accidentally making risqué jokes in front of their grandmother that had slipped past their parents' censorship.

When Fallon talks about watching and imitating *SNL* as a child, it seems as though he already knew that he was doing more than simply goofing around. A self-proclaimed "weird kid," Jimmy often spent time attending garage sales with his mother and spending his own money on odds and ends his neighbors were selling. At one garage sale, he bought a reel-to-reel tape recorder, which was a type of recording device predating the cassette tape. This technology was already outdated by the time Jimmy was a child, but he used the vintage device to make audiotapes of *SNL* monologues and sketches, and he would replay them and lip-synch

IRISH ANCESTRY

Both of Fallon's parents are of partial Irish ancestry. His father, James Thomas Fallon Sr., is Irish and German, while his mother, Gloria, is Irish and Norwegian. Jimmy Fallon is very proud of his Irish roots. At the age of two, he first began to develop his knack for doing impressions, cutting his teeth on a routine mimicking the famous Irish American actor James Cagney. His mother would have him do his Cagney impression for anyone who would listen, and it was a hit among family and friends. Fallon spoke about his Irish heritage in an interview quoted on IrishCentral.com, saying, "It's really, really great...I was very happy to be raised Irish. We grew up totally having a party—we were the Irish family. Across the street from us we had a great Italian family. Between the both of us there'd be a party every weekend."

These parties, along with other characteristics of the exuberant Irish culture, helped to nurture Fallon's gift for entertaining. "It's that Irish personality where, you know, I wasn't one of those people who needed to kiss the Blarney Stone," Fallon told Tom Rose in an interview on xfinity.com, speaking of the Irish superstition in which kissing a particular stone in the Blarney Castle, near Cork, Ireland, gives the kisser the gift of speaking eloquently. "I was kind of always talking. I came from a family of just entertaining people...They would have parties and they would sing, you know, just have a microphone set up with a reel-to-reel and some speakers and just—everyone would sing songs. Even though we weren't famous, we were a performing family, pretty much."

Jimmy had his first opportunity to visit Ireland when his sister Gloria was studying abroad on a scholarship

(continued on the next page)

The Irish rock band U2 performed on Jimmy Fallon's first episode hosting *The Tonight Show*. Fallon speaks often and proudly about his Irish ancestry.

(continued from the previous page)

at a university in London, England. Gloria won a writing contest, and as her prize, she was allowed to choose one friend to fly over for a visit. Proving how close Jimmy and Gloria are as siblings, Gloria chose her brother to be her guest. Upon her invitation, Jimmy got his first credit card and flew to England. During his visit, he and Gloria took a trip to Kinsale, Ireland. "I was just blown away by how nice and gorgeous people were," said Fallon, according to IrishCentral.com. In subsequent years, he has been back to Ireland many times.

Fallon spoke more about his Irish ancestry when Van Morrison appeared as the musical guest on Fallon's first night hosting *Late Night*. "I grew up an Irish kid and, you know, he comes on your iPod in your brain when you're born. He's just like—he's one of my favorites of all times. The fact we have Van Morrison on alone should be a shout-out to all my Irish friends going 'All right.'" The shout-out to Fallon's Irish heritage continued on the first night that Jimmy hosted *The Tonight Show*, when the musical guests were one of the most famous Irish bands of all time, U2.

them in his mirror. He preferred the reel-to-reel over the more modern cassette because cassettes would record only sixty to ninety minutes at a time, while the reel-to-reel allowed him to record for several hours. In addition to *SNL*, he would also record *The*

Dr. Demento Show, a syndicated radio broadcast featuring novelty and comedic songs by acts such as Weird Al Yankovic and Monty Python's Flying Circus. From the very beginning, Jimmy appreciated the intersection of comedy and music.

Later, when Jimmy was allowed to watch live broadcasts of *Saturday Night Live*, he insisted on watching new episodes by himself, without distractions. He told *Vanity Fair* in a 2014 interview, "I just didn't want anyone ruining my experience. No small talk. I wanted to see the sketches, the new characters, what the angle was." From the time he was a child, Jimmy always viewed comedy as a craft, studying the characters, jokes, and delivery with the eyes of an apprentice. To this day, he still watches *Saturday Night Live* with the same intensity, studying it and communicating with creator Lorne Michaels about what he sees. He has mellowed a bit on his need to watch the show alone, however, and will now watch with his wife, Nancy, and his own kids.

From Altar Boy to Class Clown

Jimmy attended a Roman Catholic grade school in Saugerties called St. Mary of the Snow, and, as he told *Spin* magazine, at one point during his childhood he wanted to be a priest: "I was pretty religious. I was an altar boy, and I was good at it. Then I started meeting girls, and I'm like, you know, maybe

I shouldn't be a priest." He spoke more about this early aspiration in an NPR interview with Terri Gross. "I loved the church," he told Gross. "...I loved the feeling you get when you left church. I love, like, how this priest could make people feel this good."

Fallon said that he genuinely felt the calling to be a priest, and Gross asked him if the calling he felt might have actually been to show business since the priest is the performer in church. Fallon said that was a possibility and that being an altar boy was absolutely his first experience of being onstage. He sometimes had a difficult time keeping a straight face at church, which foreshadowed his tendency to break character on *SNL*.

By the time he entered Saugerties High School, Jimmy's interests and aspirations leaned away from the church and more toward comedy and performing, and his sheltered upbringing did not seem to cause any problems for him socially. He was considered a class clown in high school, although teachers and administrators also found him to be a polite and well-mannered student. He was well-liked by his classmates as well, and they twice voted him social director of the class. He performed in almost every lip-synch contest and theater performance the school put on. His success in school performances led him to venture into comedy clubs by the time he was seventeen.

Leaving College and Moving to Los Angeles

When he graduated from Saugerties High, Fallon spent a few years attending the College of Saint Rose in Albany, where he was pursuing a degree in computer science. During his time in college, however, he continued to pursue his passion for performing by doing stand-up in comedy clubs. Eventually, his love for the art and his success in these small venues led him to leave the College of Saint Rose, just fifteen credits shy of earning a degree.

While serving a brief stint as a secretary for a newsweekly in Albany called *Metroland*, Fallon had met a friend who eventually left to become a manager in Los Angeles. This friend took Fallon's tape, résumé, and headshot with him and began shopping them around. Randi Siegel from the L.A. improv company the Groundlings saw Fallon's tape and invited him to work with the company. When Siegel asked him what his eventual goal was, Fallon, true to his dream, told her he aspired to be on *SNL*. She told him that he needed to pick a secondary goal, but he would not waver.

Many of the stories from Fallon's childhood, from his *SNL* impressions with his sister, to the lively, music-filled parties with his extended family, to his success with performing as a teenager, reveal his early talent for making people laugh. Fallon's close observations of *SNL* and comedy in general helped him to sharpen his wit and develop a knack for satire. Satire, a form of humor used by many of the most influential comedians, uses sarcasm, irony, and exaggeration to expose and make fun of specific shortcomings of public figures or of society in general. Satire is a key element in sketch shows like *SNL*, as well as in late-night comedic talk shows. Fallon's early development of this skill prepared him for the rest of his career.

However, the thing that set Fallon apart from the beginning was his good nature. When asked by NPR's Terri Gross why people never seem to take offense at his impressions, Fallon said, "I never kick anyone when they're down. I either kick them when they're up and they don't mind, or I don't hit them that hard, my jokes aren't that mean spirited." This is one of the things that sets Fallon's humor and satire apart from that of many of his fellow comedians.

CHAPTER
TWO

Stand-up and Other Early Work

C ritics often remark on the fact that Jimmy Fallon does not fit the stereotype of the "tortured comedian," the idea that most comedy comes from the attempt to cope with some tragedy or to gain revenge on a hostile world through humor. When Terri Gross asked him if there was anything in his past that could be construed this way, Fallon replied, "I think if I ever went to therapy you'd find something," but he went on to say that overall, his childhood was pleasant. "I mean, I got picked on like any kid would get picked on in school, but not that much. I think I had a pretty normal childhood."

This "normal" childhood set the stage for Fallon's life as a beloved, successful comedian.

However, he did not transform overnight from a sheltered kid doing impressions in the living room to a superstar on *Saturday Night Live*. The time in between his school years and his rise to fame included a lot of stand-up comedy and work with improvisational comedy troupes, often for very little pay.

Fallon began working in comedy clubs immediately following high school, while he was still attending college. He remembers his very first paid gig as a comedian but can't recall the name of the town where the playhouse was located. He drove there from Albany without telling his parents and slept in a room above the theater. He performed four sets over the weekend, two on Friday and two on Saturday. They were well received, and when the owner paid him for the gig, he said that Fallon had a future in comedy. Fallon treated himself to breakfast at a café across the street, and it was the first time he had ever paid for his own meal. "I remember getting pumpkin pancakes," he told *Vanity Fair.* "To this day, if I eat a pumpkin-flavored anything, I go back to that day, and I get emotional. Just the whole mix of everything. It was raining, and I really enjoyed myself. It was lonely but exciting at the same time. The coffee tasted extra good. And I paid for those pumpkin pancakes."

That gig was followed by many more, and Fallon began to focus more on his comedy career than

Some of Fallon's earliest stand-up performances took place on the stage of Caroline's, one of New York City's most popular comedy clubs, located in Times Square.

he did on his studies. He would often take the bus down to Manhattan to perform stand-up in comedy clubs there, particularly Caroline's in Times Square. He decided not to finish his degree and dropped out before his last semester. Fourteen years later, the College of Saint Rose awarded Fallon his bachelor's degree after the head of the communications department gave him an oral exam and determined that he had done enough in his career to make up his final few credits.

HOW FALLON OWES HIS CAREER TO A TROLL DOLL

Fallon often tells people that his career was essentially inspired by his mother and by a troll doll, a type of plastic novelty doll that was popular in the 1990s. Troll dolls were often dressed up in various costumes and given as gifts for special occasions. When Fallon graduated from high school, he was given a troll doll dressed in a cap and gown and holding a diploma. This inspired him to develop a routine that portrayed various famous people auditioning to be the spokesperson for troll dolls.

His initial performance of the routine was for an impression contest at a comedy club in Poughkeepsie called Bananas when he was seventeen. Fallon told Anderson Cooper this story, saying, "I had this troll doll that I don't know what I'm gonna do with this thing, and I go 'thank you so much,' and then my mom… heard about this impression contest on the radio in Poughkeepsie, New York, at Bananas Comedy Club, and

One of Fallon's earliest routines, and the one that gave him his first big break, consisted of impressions of different celebrities hocking troll doll toys.

she goes, 'Jimmy, you do impressions all the time when you're joking around, you should enter this contest.'" The impressions he used in the original troll doll routine included Jerry Seinfeld, who would become one of his most famous and often-used impressions, and Pee-Wee Herman. Fallon won the contest, and this inspired him to believe that he could pursue comedy professionally.

Fallon continued to riff on the troll doll routine in his stand-up even after he became an *SNL* cast member, and in 1998, he used a variation on the routine in his opening act for the Counting Crows at New York City's Hammerstein Ballroom. He impersonated various 1990s musicians auditioning to perform the jingle for a troll doll commercial, altering the lyrics of their actual songs to make them about trolls. Fallon played his own guitar, and the musicians he channeled included U2, Alanis Morissette, R.E.M., and the Counting Crows themselves.

Moving to L.A. and Joining the Groundlings

When Fallon realized that he wanted to leave college to pursue comedy full time, and he had been contacted by Randi Siegel from the Groundlings, he left New York City and moved to Los Angeles. He took classes with the Groundlings while performing for as little as $8.25 per show to make ends meet.

The Groundlings improv troupe takes its name from the term used to refer to lower-class audience members in the days of Shakespeare. While the upper classes sat on wood benches or in boxes in the Globe Theatre, where Shakespeare's plays were performed, the groundlings stood just below the stage. They were the most enthusiastic audience members, often heckling and participating in the performances. This name perfectly embodies the spirit of improv and sketch comedy.

Beginning as an informal performers' workshop, the modern-day Groundlings became an official theater company in 1974. They very quickly generated buzz in the entertainment industry, drawing the attention of popular 1970s comedians Lily Tomlin and Lorne Michaels, who produced Tomlin's TV special. In late 1974, Michaels asked Laraine Newman to be a cast member on *Saturday Night Live*, making her the first

The Groundlings improv company has launched the careers of many famous comedians, including Jimmy Fallon. Pictured here is the 2014 Groundlings troupe during a celebration of the company's fortieth anniversary.

Groundling to join the cast. Other members of the company who would eventually go on to join *SNL* include Phil Hartman, Ana Gasteyer, Will Ferrell, Chris Kattan, Maya Rudolph, Kristen Wiig, Taran Killam, and, of course, Jimmy Fallon.

The low wages for which Fallon worked while studying and performing with this troupe were offset by the value of having a chance to work and study comedy in a company that had nurtured such a large number of successful sketch comedians and had led some of them to Fallon's highest aspiration: a spot on *Saturday Night Live*. This had been a fixation for nearly as long as he could remember. "I used to pray that I'd be on it one day," he told *Spin* magazine. "I'd cut my birthday cake and wish that I was on *Saturday Night Live*. I'd see a falling star and wish I was on *Saturday Night Live*."

Fallon felt that this goal was the only important thing in his life: "I didn't have friends, I didn't have a girlfriend, I had nothing going on. I had my career, that was it." Making it onto *Saturday Night Live* would mean to Fallon that his career was truly taking off, and training with the Groundlings was bringing him one step closer to this dream.

What Is Improv?

"Improv" is short for "improvisational theater," in which the dialogue and all other aspects of the performance are created on the spot by the performers themselves. Instead of following a written script, the actors make it up as they go along, taking cues from the contributions of the other actors. This form of theater dates all the way back to the *commedia dell'arte* troupes who staged improvisational street performances in sixteenth- to eighteenth-century Italy. In the late 1800s, some of the most influential theater theorists, including Konstantin Stanislavsky and Jacques Copeau, stressed the importance of improvisation as a tool in training and rehearsal. In the twentieth century, many theater companies devoted exclusively to comedic improv began to arise. These companies include the Groundlings in L.A., the Second City in Chicago, and the Upright Citizens Brigade in New York City.

Improv has its own philosophy, developed over the course of the years in which it has been practiced. There are many lists of "rules" for improv, most of which are variations on the same basic ideas. In her book *Bossypants,* Jimmy Fallon's former *SNL* costar and "Weekend Update" coanchor, Tina Fey, provides a list of some of these fundamental commandments. Here is that list, with explanations of each rule.

> **Rule #1: Agree.** Seek to find common ground with your fellow performers, rather than blocking or shooting down their ideas.

Rule #2: Not Only Say "Yes," Say "Yes, And..." Contribute to and build upon the ideas introduced by your colleagues.

Rule #3: Make Statements. Asking questions puts the pressure back on the other performers. Making statements brings something into being and allows the scene to move forward.

Rule #4: There Are No Mistakes, Only Opportunities. When something does not go the way you expected, look for a way to lean into it and to embrace the new direction that the scene has taken.

Speaking on what made Fallon a successful improv performer, Groundlings instructor Karen Maruyama said, "Jimmy has a strong presence and energy, but he also had a vulnerability that made him endearing." Whether he is working from a script or not, Fallon's training and experience in improv very obviously influence his comedic style. His willingness to say "yes" and to embrace mistakes as opportunities is evident in the finesse with which he handles his tendency to break character, the charm with which he handles awkward moments in interviews, and the spontaneity and spark of life he brings to any role or television appearance. The philosophy of improv and its spirit of welcome probably have a lot to do with why Fallon is so well liked as a host and an interviewer and why he is so easily able to make his subjects feel comfortable.

Landing an *SNL* Audition

While studying and performing with the Groundlings, Fallon also did stand-up at L.A.'s Improv Theater, working for only $7.50 a set. During this time he was also auditioning for pilots and for guest-starring spots on various television shows. Of course, no matter what other pursuits were occupying his time, Fallon never lost sight of his primary goal, *Saturday Night Live*. His devotion was so fierce that when he landed a role in a pilot for a show on the WB network, he insisted on adding a clause to his contract that would release him if he ever got hired for *SNL*.

In 1997, when Fallon had been working with the Groundlings for two years, he got his first shot at realizing his dream: he finally landed an audition for *SNL*. In interviews, Fallon does not usually elaborate too much on this first audition, which took place in a comedy club, because it bombed. However, he did tell Terri Gross in his 2011 NPR interview that the audition consisted of his troll doll impression act, which he still often used during his stand-up routines at that time. The act was not well received, and Fallon was not hired for *SNL* that season; Tracy Morgan was chosen instead.

Fallon, depressed by this setback, returned to

L.A. and continued his work there with some success, including his first-ever TV appearance, on a
1998 episode of the sitcom *Spin City*. He played a
photographer taking pictures in line at a club and
trying to pressure people into buying them. Even
though his first audition had failed, Fallon was still
determined to get a spot on *Saturday Night Live*. His
persistence and resilience paid off when *SNL* called
and asked him to audition again. His first attempt
had apparently made a better impression than he
initially thought. However, the casting team asked
him to leave the troll doll act behind; they were
ready to see something else. Fallon got to work
revamping his material and preparing to take a second shot at his lifelong aspiration.

CHAPTER
THREE

Saturday Night Live

F allon loves to tell the story of his second audition for *SNL*, adding different details every time he recalls it. He often mentions how he was so starstruck just being in the building that he took pictures of the elevator floor, which displayed NBC's peacock logo. He was taken with the atmosphere and with the feel and even the smell of the studio itself.

"It was in Studio 8H," Fallon said of this second audition, speaking to Jonathan Durbin for *Paper* magazine, "the *SNL* soundstage. And I remember thinking that even if I didn't get hired, this was such a cool thing that it didn't matter—I could still tell my friends and family that I'd auditioned for Lorne Michaels." Fallon's audition that day still consisted of celebrity impressions, but

Jimmy Fallon poses with Lorne Michaels, one of his mentors and greatest supporters. Fallon was starstruck when he auditioned in front of Michaels for *Saturday Night Live.*

he framed the routine as a "celebrity walkathon" instead of his old troll doll routine. The audition also included demonstrations of some of the original characters he had developed, as well as musical impressions.

Fallon recalls that during the audition process, several people warned him about Lorne Michaels's legendary stone face during auditions. "The whole afternoon, people had been telling me 'Lorne doesn't laugh—he's seen it all, so don't think he doesn't think you're funny if he doesn't laugh.' It just went on and on, a huge psych-out." However, Fallon's impression of Adam Sandler, one of the show's most popular cast members, proved to be fresh enough to break Michaels's no-laughing rule. "I finished the audition with Sandler…and Lorne turned his face away, but I could see that he'd cracked up. It was such a surreal and cool moment."

Finding His Groove

As a result of that impressive audition, Fallon began his stint on *Saturday Night Live* as a featured player during the 1998–99 season. He launched many of his popular impressions and characters during his first season. The Adam Sandler impression that won him his spot on the show proved to be just as popular with viewers as it was with Lorne Michaels and the casting team.

The sketch that cemented Fallon's status as the breakout star of the season came during his fourth episode. He appeared on "Weekend Update," *SNL*'s satirical news segment, which was hosted by Colin Quinn at the time, and performed Halloween-themed parodies of popular songs by current artists, including Alanis Morissette and Counting Crows, two of his favorite musical impressions.

During his first season, he also launched the character of Nick Burns, Computer Guy, a snarky corporate IT support person who would make fun of people's lack of computer knowledge as he fixed their technical problems. Fallon originally developed this character in his classes with the Groundlings, drawing on some of his knowledge from the time he spent pursuing a computer science degree at the College of Saint Rose. Fallon told NPR's Terri Gross that although he was much nicer than Nick Burns when he worked on people's computers, Nick's tendency to tell people to move from their chairs so he could have access to their computers is something that he himself did.

Second Season: "Weekend Update" and More

During the summer of 1999, after his remarkably successful season as a featured player, Fallon was promoted to the position of full cast member. In 2000, Fallon and Tina Fey (who was a writer for *SNL* at the time but not a cast member) joined forces to audition as a replacement team for Colin Quinn, who was leaving his post as anchor of "Weekend Update." Lorne Michaels had approached Fallon and asked him to do "Update" when Quinn left, but at first, Fallon hadn't been interested. However, when he saw Tina Fey's audition, he changed his mind. Fey and Fallon had already worked together a lot, collaborating on the writing for many of Fallon's sketches. He and Fey did a test run of their version of "Weekend Update," and Michaels loved it, saying, "She's the smart one and you're the guy who forgot to do his homework and needs to cheat off her,"

Fallon with Tina Fey on the set of "Weekend Update." The two comedians made a dynamic team, and their version of "Update" was very popular with audiences.

according to Fallon in his interview with Gross. "That's the dynamic."

Fallon and Fey won out against Ana Gasteyer and Chris Parnell, who had also auditioned as coanchors. Together, they launched a new era of "Weekend Update," which included features such as the Update Door, through which cast members impersonating celebrities would appear, and Terrible Reenactments, in which Chris Kattan would intentionally butcher a reenactment of a celebrity news story from the week. Fallon and Fey's chemistry was popular with viewers, and the duo remained as "Weekend Update" hosts until Fallon left the show and was replaced by Amy Poehler.

During his second season on *SNL*, Fallon also branched out, working in other media besides television. He and his sister, Gloria, coauthored *I Hate This Place: The Pessimist's Guide to Life*, a book based on the siblings' cross-country e-mail exchanges. During the same season, Fallon also portrayed band manager Dennis Hope in the Cameron Crowe film *Almost Famous*. Like most of Fallon's cinematic ventures, the film did poorly in theaters. However, it received a lot of positive attention from critics and earned four Oscar nominations, winning Best Screenplay for writer Cameron Crowe.

In 2002, Fallon released his first comedy album, *The Bathroom Wall*. The first five tracks on the album are studio recordings of comedic songs. The second half of the album consists of live recordings of stand-up material, including the legendary troll doll celebrities and troll doll jingles routines.

Fallon's *SNL* Highlights

Like all beloved *Saturday Night Live* cast members, Jimmy Fallon's time on the show included certain characters and sketches that were especially popular with audiences. Here are a few of the highlights from Fallon's *SNL* run that have not already been discussed.

"The Boston Teens": Fallon and Rachel Dratch played Pat "Sully" Sullivan and Denise "Zazu" McDenna, two Massachusetts teenagers who constantly argued, made out, and spoke in exaggerated Boston accents.

"Jarret's Room": This sketch, reminiscent of another *SNL* classic, "Wayne's World," featured Fallon as Jarret, a stoner college student who filmed a webcast from his dorm room. His roommate Gobi, played by Horatio Sanz, was a recurring character, and the band Phish once guest-starred.

"The Barry Gibb Talk Show": Fallon portrayed Barry Gibb, the lead singer of the Bee Gees, who hosted a talk show (usually featuring political guests) in which he often angrily berated his guests and sang in an exaggeration of the his signature falsetto. Justin Timberlake costarred as Barry's brother and fellow Bee Gee, Robin Gibb.

Mick Jagger: During his time on *SNL*, Fallon was the show's most popular impressionist, mimicking stars such as Robert DeNiro, Jerry Seinfeld, and Howard Stern. One of his most popular moments as an impressionist came when Mick Jagger hosted the show. The real Jagger sat in front of a mirror in a dressing room and talked to "himself"—actually

Jimmy Fallon poses with Rolling Stones front man Mick Jagger, one of Fallon's most popular impressions on *Saturday Night Live*. Jagger himself appeared in a sketch with Fallon.

Fallon doing his Jagger impression. During the sketch, Jagger was visibly entertained, breaking character and laughing at one point. This sketch was referenced when Fallon returned to host *SNL* in 2010; he sat in front of a mirror talking to Andy Samberg doing an impression of him.

Fallon himself had a tendency to break character during *SNL* sketches, and this became a staple of his performances, something that audience members waited for and that costars sometimes intentionally tried to encourage. Some critics (and, reportedly, Lorne Michaels himself) disliked this tendency, claiming that it showed arrogance and that Fallon was trying to steal the moment from other actors in the scene. Most of the actors themselves, however, found it hilarious, including Will Ferrell, who, during a sketch that took place in a hot tub, repeatedly pinched Fallon's leg in an attempt to get him to break.

FRIENDSHIP WITH JUSTIN TIMBERLAKE

Justin Timberlake and Jimmy Fallon first met backstage at the 2002 MTV Video Music Awards. Both men were nervous that night; it was Timberlake's first televised performance as a solo artist without his former band,

(continued on the next page)

(continued from the previous page)

NSYNC, and it was Fallon's first time hosting the awards. Even ten years later, Fallon remembered the significance of this meeting in an interview with GQ, saying to Timberlake, "I remember talking backstage at those VMAs. I was totally nervous and you were nervous and we both ended up having a good night. We're good luck to each other—like each other's rabbit foots."

That meeting marked the beginning of a friendship, characterized by many as a "bromance," that has given birth to some memorable *SNL* sketches and segments of Fallon's late night shows. Many of the collaborations between Fallon and Timberlake revolve around music since both of them are talented musicians who also do excellent impressions and parodies of other musicians. Their first musical sketch together was "The Barry Gibb Talk Show" on *SNL*, where they showed off their skills at impersonating the Bee Gees' signature falsetto. The two first appeared in this sketch in 2003 when Fallon was still a cast member on *SNL*. Since Fallon left the show, the two have reprised the sketch several times when one or the other of

(continued on the next page)

Often referred to as a "bromance," Jimmy Fallon's friendship with Justin Timberlake has led to many hilarious collaborations. The two friends share a love of music and comedy and an aptitude for combining the two.

(continued from the previous page)

them is hosting. Another memorable sketch for which they teamed up was "Wrappinville" during the 2013 Christmas season, in which they portrayed "professional wrappers" who parodied popular hip-hop songs with lyrics about gift wrapping.

Timberlake was a guest on Fallon's first episode hosting *Late Night*, and the duo again demonstrated their love of hip-hop in their "History of Rap" segments on the show. In 2011, *GQ* magazine named them "Men of the Year," and in 2013, when Fallon was named one of the "100 Most Influential People" by *Time* magazine, Timberlake wrote the essay that appeared in the issue. Later the same year, the two appeared together at the VMAs again when Fallon presented Timberlake with the Michael Jackson Video Vanguard Award.

In his essay about Fallon in *Time* magazine, Timberlake shares a story that epitomizes the dynamic of their friendship, telling how Fallon interrupted an impromptu speech Timberlake was giving to his new bride, Jessica Biel, at their wedding: "I paused just for a moment in between thoughts. And then there was Jimmy, shouting a joke from his seat, sparking an improv between the two of us that went on for a good five or ten minutes and had all of our guests roaring with laughter…Anyone else would have bombed on that stage. And then I would have kicked their [butt]. But this was Jimmy Fallon. He just can't help himself. And neither can we."

Moving On

Fallon began to explore the possibility of a film career while he was still on *SNL*, reading scripts and considering roles he was offered. Although he turned down most of them, the lead role in the movie *Taxi* opposite Queen Latifah caught his interest. He began shooting the film in the fall of 2003. A remake of a 1998 French film with the same title, the movie also starred Ann-Margret and Gisele Bündchen.

In May 2004, at the end of the show's twenty-ninth season and his sixth season as a cast member, Fallon decided to leave *Saturday Night Live* to pursue a full-time career in film. Unfortunately, *Taxi*, which was released that October, was panned by critics and was only marginally financially successful. Following *Taxi*, Fallon starred opposite Drew Barrymore in *Fever Pitch,* an adaptation of a Nick Hornby novel of the same name, which did only slightly better than *Taxi*. The main upside of *Fever Pitch* was that on the set, Fallon met Drew Barrymore's business partner and coproducer Nancy Juvonen, who would eventually become his girlfriend and then his wife. However, this did not change the fact that the movie failed to meet expectations, and following these two unsuccessful films, the offers stopped coming in.

Fallon poses with his wife, film director Nancy Juvonen, whom he met on the set of *Fever Pitch*. Juvonen is business partners with Drew Barrymore, who is a good friend of the couple.

Fallon missed his *Saturday Night Live* cast mates, and he would watch the show thinking how he could have performed certain impressions and sketches he saw other people performing. This contributed to his depression about his failing movie career. Fallon has described this time as a "dark period" in his life and has mentioned Lorne Michaels, with whom he stayed in regular communication, as one of the main people who helped to pull him out of it.

Despite the apparent failure of Fallon's movie career, Michaels still had faith in his *SNL* alum. He had previously told Fallon that he thought he would be a good candidate to take over for Conan O'Brien as the host of *Late Night* when O'Brien left to host *The Tonight Show*. Although O'Brien was still hosting in 2007, Lorne Michaels convinced the producers to provide a "holding deal" so that Fallon would not be tempted into another job. This meant that NBC would pay Fallon a certain amount of money to guarantee that he would be available to take over for O'Brien when the time came. In May 2008, it was announced that O'Brien was leaving and that Fallon would take over as host of *Late Night* the following season.

Since leaving *Saturday Night Live* as a cast member, Fallon has returned twice to host the show. His first time hosting was in December 2011, with Michael Bublé as the musical guest. In December 2013, he returned, joining his close friend Justin Timberlake, who was the musical guest for that episode. Fallon and Timberlake also appeared together on the *SNL 40th Anniversary Special*, performing a musical number that paid homage to many classic *SNL* sketches.

CHAPTER **FOUR**

Late Night with Jimmy Fallon

Fallon began hosting *Late Night* in 2009. As most hosts do when they take over a show, he revamped the style and structure. Under Fallon's reign, *Late Night* transformed from a talk show into a full-fledged modern-day variety show. He expanded the traditional monologue and interview format of late night talk shows to include unprecedented emphasis on other segments, including celebrity games, comedic sketches, and musical numbers. In 2011, 2012, and 2013, *Late Night with Jimmy Fallon* was nominated for the Emmy Award for outstanding variety series, although it was beaten out by Jon Stewart and Stephen Colbert's satirical news shows, *The Daily Show*

and *The Colbert Report.*
However, Fallon won an
Emmy in 2010 for the show's
social media presence and
website, and he also won
two consecutive People's
Choice Awards for favorite
late night talk show host.

Fallon has mentioned that
his experience on "Weekend
Update" was very helpful in
preparing him to be a talk
show host because it gave
him practice playing himself
rather than doing impres-
sions or playing characters.
Still, he went through a
period of adjustment when
he began hosting *Late Night.*
Although the sketches,
games, and musical num-
bers came very naturally to
Fallon, the interview segments were much harder. He
spoke to Terri Gross about
the difficulty of interviewing, saying, "It's hard, and
I think the best advice you can give to somebody
who's getting into it is, you won't learn how to do it

Actor Robert DeNiro was the first guest on *Late Night with Jimmy Fallon*. He proved to be a difficult interview, giving short answers that did not invite follow-up questions.

until you do it." Jimmy tried practicing on his wife, Nancy, sitting to the left of her during dinner and interviewing her about her food. He also tried interviewing his mom, who he says was an awful guest; she kept insisting that he cut to a clip, which he obviously didn't have.

Despite his attempts to practice, Fallon basically had to learn how to interview on air. His first guest on *Late Night*, Robert DeNiro, did not make this easy. He responded to Fallon's questions with single-syllable answers and shrugs. Fallon was thrown for a short time and almost let his nerves get the best of him, but he recovered with something soundly in his wheelhouse: a DeNiro impression. This drew the audience back in, restoring Fallon's confidence, and although he had yet to master the art of interviewing, he rarely faltered for the rest of the episode. It helped that one of the other guests was his good friend Justin Timberlake, with whom he always has excellent comedic chemistry. Throughout the course of *Late Night with Jimmy Fallon*'s run, Fallon became much more comfortable as an interviewer and hosted many notable celebrities and politicians.

Notable Guests

Fallon's connections at *SNL* and through his film work helped him to get many prominent guests to appear even in his earliest episodes as host of *Late Night*. These guests included his old "Weekend Update" partner, Tina Fey; his *Fever Pitch* costar, Drew Barrymore; and musician Jon Bon Jovi.

As the show picked up momentum and began to draw more attention, Fallon began to draw other big names, whether or not he had previous connections with them. In addition to hosting musical guests and pop-culture icons, Fallon also hosted many politicians on *Late Night*. Fallon's interviews with political figures helped to humanize these politicians and to make them accessible to the public, whether audiences agreed or disagreed with their political positions. More than once, Fallon hosted New Jersey governor Chris Christie, with whom he had a great rapport. The two share a love of Bruce Springsteen, and in one of Christie's appearances, he and Fallon did a duet of "Thunder Road" accompanied by the Roots.

His most prominent political guest, President Barack Obama, was also arguably his most entertaining. President Obama participated in one of Fallon's regular segments, "Slow Jam the News," creating one of the most viral videos ever to arise from *Late Night with Jimmy Fallon*. The subject of the segment was President Obama's attempt to get Republicans on board with preventing an increase in student loan interest rates. Both Obama and Fallon

President Barack Obama appeared on "Slow Jam the News," one of the most popular segments of *Late Night*. This clip allowed the president to show his sense of humor, and it went viral on the Internet.

spoke about the issue while the Roots played in the background and Tariq "Black Thought" Trotter sang lines like, "If Congress doesn't act it's the students who'll pay/The right and left should join on this like Kim and Kanye." The clip was an immediate hit and, of course, went viral.

Social Media and Internet Presence

The Obama "Slow Jam the News" clip epitomizes the success of the viral video segments that were released after the network broadcasts of *Late Night with Jimmy Fallon* episodes. This was just one aspect of the show's web presence. In addition to these viral segments, which were shared across social media networks, the show had

a website that drew major traffic, and Fallon established a strong social media presence for himself, particularly on Twitter. Both the website and Fallon's Twitter presence predated the show itself, helping to generate buzz before the first episode even aired.

Perhaps the most controversial moment in Fallon's career as a talk show host also illustrates the importance of social media to the show—and demonstrates how the viral nature of clips and information can be as harmful as they can be helpful. This moment occurred in 2011, when Republican presidential candidate Michelle Bachmann walked out for her interview. As Questlove explains in his book *Mo' Meta Blues: The World According to Questlove*, this moment, called the "walkover," is one of the band's few opportunities for spontaneity during the show. Since the days of Paul Shaffer on David Letterman's show, this moment has been

During her 2011 presidential campaign, Michelle Bachmann appeared on *Late Night*. The Roots' choice of music while she walked out led to a big controversy, but it eventually blew over.

used by house bands as a time to pull out obscure musical references and make sly, difficult-to-catch jokes. For Bachmann's walkover, Questlove chose a song by rock band Fishbone, the title of which referred to his belief (shared by many of her critics) that Bachmann told lies on the campaign trail. Because the song's title was vulgar and contained a word that was perceived as both insulting and sexist, this song choice created a firestorm on Twitter and other social media that resulted in Fallon having to apologize publicly to Bachmann and almost led to the Roots being fired from the show. Luckily, the Thanksgiving weekend and a political blunder by Bachmann diffused the controversy and it blew over, but from then on the Roots' walkover song choices had to be preapproved.

WE LOVE YOU, JIMMY, OH YES WE DO...

Jimmy Fallon is extraordinarily popular not only with audiences, but also with his coworkers and fellow celebrities. It is rare that a celebrity is so universally loved by his peers, but Fallon's playfulness and welcoming affability make it difficult to dislike him. While some comedians seem to aim to alienate themselves from audiences and interview subjects, Fallon seems to aim for the opposite; he looks for common ground. The goal of his comedy is, very simply, to make people smile, and he does this by creating an environment of inclusion. This may be the reason that so many celebrities agree to appear on his show and to participate in his ideas for parodies and sketches: with Fallon, there is very little fear of being ambushed or blindsided.

Here is what some of Fallon's famous friends have to say about him.

Questlove: It hadn't even been ten minutes, and he was already able to get everybody loose and joking—no small feat, since we were a fairly guarded band. From that very first meeting, Jimmy has the ability to turn us all into thirteen-year-olds. The spirit of J. M. Barrie [the author of *Peter Pan*] is in him.

Tina Fey: Jimmy actually likes talking to people, and that's a little bit of a rarity. I think it's sort of an Irish trait with him. If you walk down the street with Jimmy, you won't go straight from Point A to Point B because he'll be stopping and talking to everyone.

Jerry Seinfeld: When you're around Jimmy, you're having a good time, I don't care who you are.

Justin Timberlake: Jimmy has redefined and recharged late-night television with a genuine

(continued on the next page)

(continued from the previous page)

excitement and energy that gets under your skin. That's probably because watching you laugh might be the thing that makes Jimmy most happy...Jimmy's lightning wit—mixed with a kindness you don't normally find in comedy—is what makes you feel so comfortable having him in your home every night. And no matter where the joke goes, the audience feels like they are in on it, too. That's because Jimmy loves to share the moment.

Drew Barrymore (on characters like Fallon's in *Fever Pitch*): They have a certain playful quality about them and I think that Jimmy totally embodies that. He's just a lovely, lovely human being. I was excited to see him in something that was romantic and more dramatic than anything he's had the chance to do yet. I really believed in him and he just did an incredible job.

Randi Siegel, former manager: He's so genuinely in awe of everyone who was on [SNL] before him. That's what's so endearing about him. His impressions aren't mean-spirited— they're a tribute to the people he grew up admiring.

Thank You Notes

Among the most successful segments introduced on *Late Night* was Fallon's "Thank You Notes," which, as he told Terri Gross, started because he wanted a signature segment like David Letterman's "Top Ten List" or Jay Leno's "Headlines." Early on in the show, Fallon was trying out different things and "spitballing" with writers to try to find something that would work. Writer Jeremy Bronson suggested that he do a bit in which he would write thank you notes to celebrities who had screwed up during the week. Fallon liked the idea, but instead of writing to celebrities, he wanted to write to mundane, everyday things or occurrences that bothered him instead. They tried it the next Friday, and the response on social media let them know that it worked. In 2011, Fallon published a volume of *Thank You Notes* in book form, and in 2012, he published a second volume.

Here are a few of the funniest notes featured in the books:

"Thank you, the word moist, for being the worst word ever. I think I speak for all Americans when I say, we don't want you as a word anymore. God I hate you."

"Thank you, hard taco shells, for surviving the long journey from factory to supermarket to my plate, and then breaking the moment I put something inside you."

"Thank you, slow walking family walking in front of me on the sidewalk, no please, take your

"Thank You Notes," a bit of *Late Night* that Fallon developed to be his signature segment, led to two different compilations in book form.

time. And definitely, spread out, too, so you can create a barricade of idiots. I'm so thankful that you forced me to walk in the street and risk getting hit by a car in order to pass you so that I could resume walking at a normal human pace."

Fallon told NPR's Terri Gross that "Thank You Notes" is a good outlet for all of the random everyday occurrences that you think "there should be a joke about that." These moments also served as the basis for many of the jokes on the classic New York sitcom *Seinfeld*, and this aspect of Fallon's comedy further characterizes him as a New York comedian.

The Roots and the Importance of Music on *Late Night*

One of the most innovative changes Fallon introduced to *Late Night* was to land the Roots as the house band for the show. By the time they joined *Late Night*, the Roots were cemented in musical history as hip-hop legends. They were the first full-fledged band in hip-hop history, the first crew to not only rap over beats, but also to create all of their own instrumentation.

A legendary hip-hop act becoming the house band for a late night TV show seems like an unlikely scenario, and initially, the Roots were not

The Roots served as the house band for *Late Night with Jimmy Fallon* and then accompanied Fallon on his move to *The Tonight Show*. The band has been essential to the vibe of both shows and to many of the musical segments.

enthusiastic about the request. In his 2013 book *Mo' Meta Blues: The World According to Questlove*, the Roots' drummer and co-front man Amir "Questlove" Thompson says that at first, he planned to decline Fallon's invitation. That changed, however, when he invited Fallon to one of the band's shows and brought him backstage to hang out. Like almost everyone who meets Fallon, the Roots were drawn in by his infectious, fun-loving nature. When Questlove rejoined the band backstage after an interview, he found Fallon and "almost the whole band—Tariq, Tuba, Owen, Frank, Kamal and others—making a huge human pyramid." He says that at the time, the band was already beginning to embrace a more fun-loving spirit, and "Jimmy brought all of that to a boil, in the best sense. I couldn't help but laugh at how silly they all looked. Oh [shoot], I thought to myself. We're stuck with this guy, aren't we?"

The Roots' presence helped to set the stage for the importance of music in Fallon's format. They were able to accompany the many musical sketches and segments that Fallon introduced, such as "Slow Jam the News," and to play along when Fallon did musical impressions.

Early on, Fallon introduced his Neil Young impression to the *Late Night* audience, and one of the show's most memorable moments came when Fallon, as Young, did a duet with Bruce Springsteen covering Willow Smith's hit song "Whip My Hair Back and Forth." One of Fallon's writers originally made the suggestion that Fallon cover the song as Young. Fallon knew that Springsteen was coming on the show, and he decided that he wanted to incorporate him into the idea. Fallon and the writer practiced the song (with the writer doing a Springsteen impression), recorded it, and sent it to Springsteen's manager.

As it turned out, Springsteen loved Fallon's Neil Young impression, his kids loved "Whip My Hair Back and Forth," and he was totally on board. He even elaborated on the idea, suggesting that he dress as 1970s Springsteen and bring his actual sunglasses from his Born to Run tour. Fallon pushed for him to wear a wig, and although Springsteen was initially reluctant, he eventually loved it. This performance created yet another viral video clip for the show. In addition to showcasing the Roots and creating viral musical segments, *Late Night* also served as the first network TV appearance for many bands and musical artists including Frank Ocean, Odd Future, Kendrick Lamar, Beach House, Grimes, Ed Sheeran, and Sam Smith.

Transitioning from *Late Night* to *The Tonight Show*

During the years that he hosted *Late Night*, Fallon also engaged in some other pursuits. In 2010, he hosted the 62nd Primetime Emmy Awards to rave reviews. In 2012, he released his second comedy album, *Blow Your Pants Off*. From 2012 to 2013, he served as creator, writer, and executive producer of an original sitcom, *Guys with Kids*, which unfortunately lasted just one season. By the end of 2013, he was preparing to hand *Late Night* over to Seth Meyers and to move on to *The Tonight Show*.

Fallon shot the last episode of *Late Night* on February 7, 2014. The final episode drew the highest ratings of the show's run. In the final segment,

Fallon performed the Band's "The Weight" along with the Muppets, singing the first verse himself and drumming along through the rest of the song. He looked wistful throughout the performance, and the emotion of the moment was palpable as he ended the song, got up, and walked silently out of the studio. However, the sadness didn't last long; he walked down the hall to a pair of doors bearing the logo for *The Tonight Show Starring Jimmy Fallon* and walked through those doors to be greeted by a cheering crowd.

The Tonight Show Starring Jimmy Fallon

T he night before Fallon bid his farewell to
Late Night and walked through the doors of *The
Tonight Show* studio, Jay Leno had hosted his
final episode of *The Tonight Show*, bidding the
audience a tearful good-bye but also expressing
his confidence that it was time to pass the torch
and that Fallon was the right person to receive it.
The stage was set for Fallon to take over as the
next host of the show, which had a tumultuous
history.

After Johnny Carson retired in 1992, Jay Leno
was brought on as an interim host, but he ended
up with the job permanently. David Letterman,
who was at the time hosting *Late Night*, had
been Carson's first choice for the job. When he
didn't get it, he left the network, making room for

Fallon's *Late Night* predecessor, Conan O'Brien. In 2009, NBC tried to put O'Brien in as the new host of *The Tonight Show*, moving Jay Leno into a prime-time spot, but due to a domino effect from poor ratings for Leno's new show, the whole setup failed. Leno was reinstated as host of *The Tonight Show*, and Jimmy Fallon became the new host of *Late Night*, where he remained until Leno retired in 2014.

Unlike some of *The Tonight Show*'s previous hosts, Jimmy Fallon did not actively aspire to host the show. Although he had dreamed of being cast on *SNL*, and although his destiny as a late night talk show host was foreshadowed when his classmates voted him most likely to fill David Letterman's shoes, he had never considered taking over *The Tonight Show* until he was approached about it. In his mind, the show was something legendary, and hosting it had never occurred to him when he was younger. However, his years on *Late Night* had groomed him well for the job, giving him the practice he needed as an interviewer and allowing him to develop his own style and identity as a host.

Return to New York

With Fallon as host, *The Tonight Show*, which had been filmed in California since 1972, returned not only to its original home city of New York, but also to its original studio home in Rockefeller Center, Studio

The Comcast Building at 30 Rockefeller Center, commonly known as "30 Rock," houses Studio 6B, where *The Tonight Show* is filmed.

6B, where Fallon had filmed *Late Night with Jimmy Fallon* for most of its run. Both Johnny Carson, the show's longest-running host, and Jack Paar, who hosted before him, had appeared from Studio 6B prior to the show's move to Los Angeles. Not only was it Fallon's birthplace, it was also the original studio of *The Tonight Show* itself. This gave some added poignancy to the show's return to New York; with Fallon's installation as host and his ties to New York City, the show was returning to its roots.

In addition to bringing *The Tonight Show* back to New York, Fallon infused it with the same fresh, young sensibility that he had injected into *Late Night*, which was much needed after Jay Leno's twenty-two-year run. He brought with him his social media savvy and his gift for creating viral videos, and he even brought some specific elements of *Late Night* along with him, including the Roots as the house band and the popular "Thank You Notes" segment.

Spike Lee directed the opening sequence, which showed Fallon visiting New York landmarks such as Katz's Deli and Grand Central Station, and introduced the show's new logo, which shows the title set against a full moon. The Roots continue to provide the same authentic and innovative musical presence they brought to *Late Night*, and musical performances and parodies are as important to Fallon's comedy as they have always been.

The *Saved by the Bell* Reunion

One of the recurring elements in Fallon's shows is his love for nostalgia of the 1990s. This love reached its greatest height when Fallon managed to assemble most of the cast of *Saved by the Bell*, an immensely popular TV show of the 1990s, for a reunion segment on *The Tonight Show*. Fallon had been dreaming about creating this reunion for a long time before it became a reality. He originally introduced the idea on *Late Night*, very early on in the show.

It began to pick up more traction when Mark-Paul Gosselaar, the star of *Saved by the Bell,* appeared on *Late Night*. He had read on the Internet about Fallon's idea for a reunion, and he had mixed feelings. However, he decided that as an experiment, he would come on the show in character as Zack Morris. This segment, in which he made many references to favorite tropes from *Saved by the Bell*, including Zack's ability to freeze time and his use of a giant, '80s-style cell phone, proved to be a huge hit with viewers. During the interview, "Zack" agreed to do the reunion and also spoke to "Jessie Spano" (Elizabeth Berkley) on the phone, getting her on board. However, it wasn't until years later, when Fallon had moved on to *The Tonight Show*, that this reunion finally became a reality.

Fallon and cast members from Saturday morning favorite *Saved by the Bell,* which Jimmy Fallon loved, do a segment on *The Tonight Show* after Fallon organized a reunion.

On the February 4, 2015, episode of *The Tonight Show*, the eight-minute reunion segment finally aired. It featured several of the former *Saved by the Bell* cast members: Gosselaar (Zack), Berkley (Jessie), Mario Lopez (A. C. Slater), Tiffani-Amber Thiessen (Kelly Kapowski), and Dennis Haskins (Principal Richard Belding). The reunion segment flawlessly recreated the feel and look of the original Saturday morning show and was full of references to favorite moments, such as Slater's ballet dancing and Jessie's caffeine-pill-induced freak-out, in which she screamed "I'm so excited, I'm so excited, I'm so...scared!"

In the segment, all of the former cast members joked not only about their *Saved by the Bell* days, but also about their subsequent careers. Fallon himself was incorporated into the sketch, which imagined that he too was a student at Bayside High but was planning to leave and move to New York to pursue a career in comedy and a spot on *Saturday Night Live*.

The reunion was a huge hit, going viral online after it aired on television. The segment realized a long-time dream for Fallon, delighted an entire generation of 1990s nostalgia junkies, and proved once again Fallon's uncanny ability to draw celebrities together and to allow them a reprieve from taking themselves too seriously.

NANCY AND JIMMY

Throughout the whirlwind of his later career, including the disappointing performance of his movies, his rise to success on *Late Night*, and his move to *The Tonight Show*, Fallon's wife, Nancy Juvonen, has been beside him. Fallon met Juvonen in 2005 on the set of *Fever Pitch*, where she was working as his costar Drew Barrymore's business partner and coproducer. Fallon noticed Juvonen as a "cute girl on the set," and the two spent some time hanging out together during production, but they kept things professional while the movie was filming.

However, months later when the movie was released, they met again while they were in London promoting the film. Fallon told Juvonen that he missed hanging out with her, and she said that she missed hanging out with him, too. From there, they started dating and fell in love. They were married in December 2007 on a private island in the Caribbean, with only family members and Drew Barrymore as guests.

Juvonen told Brian Hiatt of *Rolling Stone*, "Making comedies, you end up meeting people that you would swear would be the funnest people in the whole world, and they're not. They're really mean and depressed and hideous people. But Jimmy sees life as an opportunity and happiness as a choice. He's cheery in the morning. He wakes up happy. He gets the joke of life." Fallon and Juvonen share a love of bad reality TV like *Jersey Shore* and the *Real Housewives* shows, which Fallon told Terri Gross that the two record and watch together in the rare time they get to spend alone at home.

The couple has two daughters, Winnie and Frances, only a year apart, who were both born through a surrogate. Juvonen and the girls are the only people with whom Jimmy will break his rule of watching *SNL* alone. They also have a golden retriever named Gary Frick, who has appeared on TV with Fallon. In 2005, Fallon ventured into children's literature with a picture book called *Snowball Fight!*, illustrated by Adam Stower. His latest book, *Your Baby's First Word Will Be Dada*, illustrated by Miguel Ordoñez, was published in June 2015.

Early Reviews

Fallon's *Tonight Show* legacy remains to be determined. His predecessor, Jay Leno, hosted the show for twenty-two years, and Johnny Carson before him hosted for thirty. However, in the short time that Fallon has filled their shoes, he has received plenty of accolades. The ratings of the show have increased significantly from what they were during the last years of Leno's run, and Fallon has, unsurprisingly, drawn in a large number of younger viewers. In his first four months, ratings among eighteen- to forty-nine-year-olds (a coveted demographic) increased by 34 percent.

The first episode was reviewed widely, and those reviews were generally favorable. *New York Times* reviewer Alessandra Stanley referred to Fallon as "the grateful heir, the eager freshman, the class clown with top grades and a good heart, someone older viewers can embrace without fear of being mocked or overlooked." Some other reviewers thought that Leno's audience might have a difficult time accepting Fallon, but still their reviews were largely positive, their greatest criticism being that he was eager to be accepted. After the initial year, *Entertainment Weekly* reviewed the show, saying, "In his first year as host of 'The Tonight Show,' [Fallon] turned the revered late-night franchise into the hottest party in town, a celebrity playpen full of games, music, surprise guests, and good vibes all around."

Jay Leno himself appeared as a guest on *The Tonight Show Starring Jimmy Fallon* in November 2014, and Fallon asked him very directly, "How am I doing?" Leno jokingly tried to change the subject, saying, "Boy, it's that crisp New York weather...," but the easy rapport with which he spoke to Fallon

Fallon plays bumper cars with Jay Leno, his predecessor on *The Tonight Show*. Leno appeared as a guest on the show on one of Fallon's early episodes as host.

showed that he felt comfortable being a guest with Fallon as host. While the show is still finding its footing, Fallon is settling in, and Lorne Michaels expects him to be at *The Tonight Show* for the long haul. "There is no job for Jimmy after this," *Vanity Fair* quotes Michaels as saying. "You can't go back to being Uncle Bob in the movie. This is a different thing, something that only a few people in the world ever get to do."

COMEDIANS IN *CARS GETTING COFFEE*

One of the best examples of Fallon's rapport with other celebrities, and especially with other comedians, is the episode of Jerry Seinfeld's *Comedians in Cars Getting Coffee* that features Fallon. The show's premise is that in each episode, beloved comedian Jerry Seinfeld chooses a different vintage car in which to drive around with a selected comedian, eventually winding up at a previously chosen restaurant for coffee and sometimes food.

In Fallon's episode, Seinfeld drives, in his own description, "a 1956 Chevrolet Corvette convertible in cascade green, with beige coves and interior." In the opening montage, Seinfeld explains that he thought the optimism and positive spirit of this car made it a perfect fit for Fallon, whom he calls "the irrepressibly enjoyable host of NBC's *Tonight Show*." Upon seeing the car, Fallon says "It's a beautiful thing. This is just gorgeous. And the color. What happened with cars? Where did they stop making colors like this?" Then Fallon and Seinfeld together ask, "Why did people stop having fun?"

The two comedians ride off in the car and proceed to defy that notion by having fun for the entirety of their day together, at different points trading the Corvette for a boat and for a 1994 Land Rover Defender. Eventually, they wind up at their destination restaurant, John's Pancake House in Montauk, New York. Fallon orders

(continued on the next page)

Jimmy Fallon chats with Jerry Seinfeld. Fallon was the guest on one of the most popular episodes of Seinfeld's show *Comedians in Cars Getting Coffee.*

(continued from the previous page)

the pancakes and at one point during the meal, he tells Seinfeld that he was watching *Saturday Night Live* the previous night. Seinfeld jokes with him about how literal he is, actually watching *SNL* on Saturday night and ordering pancakes at John's Pancake House.

When the two comedians leave the pancake house in the convertible, the battery dies and they need a jump. Seinfeld is annoyed, but in a demonstration of the way that people generally feel about Fallon, he remarks how Fallon's spirit helps him to deal with the situation better. "I'm glad I'm with you," he says. "You know why? You bring out my good side. I have a dark side, but I can't have it around you." Instead of simply accepting this as a compliment, in response, Fallon displays his innate ability to put people at ease and to find common ground, telling Seinfeld how he was actually annoyed with the situation, too. Seinfeld says, "Finally, Jimmy Fallon gets annoyed. That makes my day."

At the very beginning of his time on *The Tonight Show*, Fallon remarked on his satisfaction with his life. "I'm surrounded by good people," he said. "We have a baby now. We're in New York. Lorne is in the building. And I get to ride into the sunset with these people? This is it." Now, Fallon has another baby and a successful season of *The Tonight Show Starring Jimmy Fallon* under his belt. The kid with the desperate desire to be on *Saturday Night Live* has grown up and found his niche.

Essentially, however, Fallon is still the same person he was as a kid performing in his living room in Saugerties, as a young adult hitting the comedy clubs with his troll doll routine, and during his tenure on *Saturday Night Live* and on *Late Night*. He retains his sincere, optimistic nature and outlook. He is as serious about and focused on his craft as ever, constantly coming up with innovative ways to share his comedy. He is an unabashed lover and performer of music. He is a New Yorker, raising his family in the city where he was born and to which he brought back *The Tonight Show*. And most of all, he is joyfully playful and intent on drawing everyone, guests and viewers alike, into that joy.

Fact Sheet ON JIMMY FALLON

Full Name: James Thomas Fallon Jr.
Birthplace: Brooklyn, NY
Birthdate: September 19, 1974
Siblings: Older sister, Gloria
Current Residence: New York, NY
Childhood Aspiration: To be on *Saturday Night Live*
Grade School Attended: St. Mary of the Snow
High School Attended: Saugerties High School
College Attended: The College of Saint Rose
First Performance: Theater in high school
First Paying Performance: At a comedy club in upstate New York at age seventeen
Family: Married to Nancy Juvonen and has two daughters, Winnie and Frances
Pets: Gary Frick, a female golden retriever
Instruments Played: Guitar and harmonica

Fact Sheet <u>ON JIMMY FALLON'S WORK</u>

Comedy Troupes
1995–1998   The Groundlings in L.A.

Television Credits
1998   *Spin City*, "The Marrying Men," Photographer

1998–2004   *Saturday Night Live*, 120 episodes, himself/various characters

2001   *Band of Brothers*, "Crossroads," Second Lieutenant George Rice

2001, 2005   MTV Movie Awards, host

2002   MTV Video Music Awards, host

2003   *Late Show with David Letterman*, guest host

2009, 2012   *30 Rock*, three episodes, himself

2009–2014   *Late Night with Jimmy Fallon*, host

2009   *The Electric Company*, eight episodes, himself

2009   *Sesame Street*, "Wild Nature Survivor Guy," Wild Nature Survivor Guy

2009   *Family Guy*, "We Love You Conrad," himself (voice)

2009   *Gossip Girl, "The Grandfather: Part II,"* himself

2010   62nd Primetime Emmy Awards, host

2010   *Delocated*, "Kim's Crafts," himself

2011, 2013   *Saturday Night Live*, two episodes, host

2011   *Silent Library*, "Jimmy Fallon/The Roots," himself

2012   *iCarly*, "iShock America," himself

2012–2013   *Guys with Kids*, seventeen episodes, creator, writer, executive producer

2014–Present   *The Tonight Show Starring Jimmy Fallon*, host

2015   *Louie*, "A La Carte," himself

Film Credits

2000   *Almost Famous*, Dennis Hope

2002   *The Rutles 2: Can't Buy Me Lunch,* Reporter

2003   *Anything Else*, Bob

2003   *The Entrepreneurs*, Ray

2004   *Taxi*, Detective Andy Washburn

2005   *Fever Pitch*, Ben Wrightman

2006   *Doogal*, Dylan (voice)

2006   *Arthur and the Invisibles*, Prince Betemeche (voice)

2006   *Factory Girl*, Chuck Wein

2008   *The Year of Getting to Know Us*, Christopher Rocket

2009   *Whip It*, Johnny Rocket

2009   *Arthur and the Revenge of Maltazard*, Prince Betameche (voice)

2010   *Arthur 3: The War of the Two Worlds*, Prince Betameche (voice)

2011   *Bucky Larson: Born to Be a Star*, himself, cameo

2015   *Jurassic World*, himself, cameo

Discography

The Bathroom Wall, Dreamworks, 2002
Blow Your Pants Off, Warner Brothers, 2012
"Car Wash for Peace," 2007
"Drunk on Christmas," 2009
"EW!" feat. will.i.am, 2014

Books

Snowball Fight! Illustrated by Adam Stower. New
    York, NY: Dutton Books, 2005.
I Hate This Place: The Pessimist's Guide to Life.
    Written with Gloria Fallon. New York, NY: Grand
    Central Publishing, 2008.
*Thank You Note*s. New York, NY: Grand Central
    Publishing, 2011.
Thank You Notes 2. New York, NY: Grand Central
    Publishing, 2012.
Your Baby's First Word Will Be Dada. Illustrated
    by Miguel Ordoñez. New York, NY: Feiwel and
    Friends, 2015.

Critical Reviews

"In the relative safety of his 12:35 a.m. time slot, Fallon has been cultivating a distinct, and refreshing, strain of humor: the comedy of unabashed celebration. If other late-night shows have come to feature a familiar crankiness—directed at politicians, our trashy culture, or rival talk-show hosts—Fallon, by contrast, now presides over a goofy, raucous, playful, innovative hour of shameless shenanigans."
—Adam Sternbergh, *New York* magazine, on *Late Night with Jimmy Fallon*

"Since this time last year, *The Tonight Show* has exploded from 514,000 to 1.8 million Twitter followers; on Facebook, it went from 765,000 to 4 million followers; and on YouTube, it rose from 1.5 million to 5.2 million subscribers. That's enough to eclipse every other late-night host from Jimmy Kimmel to David Letterman. Thanks to Fallon, *The Tonight Show* has gone viral."
—Ray Rahman, *Entertainment Weekly*

"With help from his secret weapon, house band the Roots…Fallon became the most retweeted, most Hulu-ed, most TiVo-ed man in late night. He's also a new breed of talk-show host: He sings…; he dances; he impersonates Neil Young; he stars in a serial vampire parody called 'Suckers'; he plays

beer pong with Betty White; he spends more time thinking about three-minute viral clips than TV ratings."
—Brian Hiatt, *Rolling Stone*

"Fallon's appeal is how earnest and energetic he is: the king of comedic kindness. He has an infectious enthusiasm not marred by any of the edge or irony of other late night stalwarts. Fallon is always happy to be there, always happy that his guests are there, and always happy you are there, too."
—Willa Paskin, *Slate*

"He was the grateful heir, the eager freshman, the class clown with top grades and a good heart, someone older viewers can embrace without fear of being mocked or overlooked."
—Alessandra Stanley, *New York Times*, on Fallon's first episode of *The Tonight Show*

Timeline

1974 Jimmy Fallon is born in Brooklyn, New York.

1976 The Fallon family moves to Saugerties, New York.

1987 Jimmy begins playing guitar.

1992 Jimmy graduates from Saugerties High School.

1995 Fallon moves to Los Angeles and begins working with the Groundlings.

1997 Fallon auditions for *Saturday Night Live* for the first time and is not cast.

1998 Fallon auditions for *SNL* again and wins a spot.

1999 Fallon and his sister, Gloria, publish *I Hate This Place: A Pessimist's Guide to Life.*

2000 Fallon becomes coanchor of "Weekend Update." *Almost Famous* is released.

2002 Fallon releases his first comedy album, *The Bathroom Wall.*

2004 Fallon leaves *SNL*. *Taxi* is released.

2005 *Fever Pitch* is released.

2007 Fallon marries Nancy Juvonen.

2009 Fallon begins hosting *Late Night with Jimmy Fallon.*

2010 Fallon hosts the 62nd Annual Emmy Awards.

2012 Fallon releases his second comedy album, *Blow Your Pants Off.*

2013 Fallon's daughter Winnie is born.

2014 Fallon begins hosting *The Tonight Show*. His daughter Frances is born.

Glossary

apprentice Someone who is formally and seriously learning a trade.

breaking In acting, when an actor comes out of character by laughing or noticeably forgetting lines.

bromance A close, affectionate, platonic bond between two men.

clause In a legal document, a distinct provision.

construe To understand the meaning of something in a particular way.

eloquent Well-spoken.

epitomize To be the perfect example or representation of something.

firestorm An intense, negative response.

foreshadow To hint at something before it actually occurs.

groundlings In Shakespeare's day, lower-class members of the audience who stood in the pit in front of the stage.

holding deal When a network pays a performer to stay available until a prospective project begins.

idyllic Simple, peaceful.

improv A type of theater, most often comic, done without a script and improvised while it is performed.

inaugural Marking the very beginning of something; the first.

interim Temporary, in the meantime.

irony The use of words to mean something different from (usually opposite of) their literal meaning.

mundane Boring, common.

nuance A subtle difference in meaning, tone, or feeling.

parody A musical, literary, or other artistic work that imitates the style and structure of another work in order to poke fun at it.

rapport Relationship or connection, such as a teacher with his students or a performer with her audience.

reprieve A temporary rest or relief.

revamp To change or reinvent something

riff To repeat, with variations, a particular theme, phrase, or idea.

satire Using irony and witty humor to expose the flaws of individuals and societies.

savvy Knowledgeable, well-informed, and perceptive, usually in regard to a particular subject (e.g. tech-savvy, media-savvy).

subsequent Happening after something else; coming later in a sequence of events.

tumultuous Chaotic, disorderly.

vignette A short, impressionistic scene in literature or theater.

viral A video, article, or meme that appears suddenly all over the Internet, the way a virus does in the body.

voracious Having a huge appetite for something.

walkover The song played by the house band while a talk show guest walks out to be interviewed.

wheelhouse The enclosed area on a boat or ship from which someone steers. The expression "in someone's wheelhouse" means within one's area of expertise.

For More Information

Canadian Improv Games
135 Séraphin-Marion
Ottawa, ON K1N 6N5
Canada
(613) 726-6339 (613-7COMEDY)
Website: http://improv.ca
Since 1977, the Canadian Improv Games have
gathered high school students all over Canada
to explore improvisation in a supportive setting.
The organization offers training in addition to
organizing competitions.

Cherub Improv
c/o Vandenburg and Feliu LLP
60 East 42nd Street, 51st Floor
New York, NY 10165
(212) 243-7824
Website: http://www.cherubimprov.org
Cherub Improv uses improv comedy as a way to help
people in need. The group works with homeless
shelters, senior centers, homes for runaway
children, and other organizations to teach short-
form improv and musical improv comedy.

Comedy Cures Foundation
122 E. Clinton Avenue
Tenafly, NJ 07670
(201) 227-8410
Website: http://www.comedycures.org

Founded by cancer survivor Saranne Rothberg, the
Comedy Cures Foundation brings comedy,
through both entertainment and education, to
children and adults suffering from illness,
depression, disabilities, and other traumas.

The Groundlings
7307 Melrose Avenue
Los Angeles, CA 90046
(323) 934-4747
Website: http://www.groundlings.com
Delighting Los Angeles audiences for more than
thirty-six years, this nonprofit organization
stages performances and offers improv training
for aspiring comedians. It has launched many
successful stars including Kristen Wiig, Maya
Rudolph, and Jimmy Fallon.

Second City Toronto
51 Mercer Street
Toronto, ON M5V 9G9
Canada
(416) 343-0011
Website: http://www.secondcity.com/shows/toronto
An offshoot of the original Chicago location, the
Second City in Toronto produces improv shows
and offers classes for both children and adults.
The Second City organization has trained many
famous and successful comedians.

Upright Citizens Brigade (UCB)
153 E. 3rd Street
New York, NY 10009
(212) 366-9176
Website: http://www.ucbtheater.com
Like The Groundlings and Second City, UCB offers
    both performances and training classes in
    improv. From 1998 to 2000, UCB (Amy Poehler,
    Matt Besser, Ian Roberts, and Matt Walsh) had
    a show on Comedy Central. During this time,
    they founded the UCB Theater, which now has
    two locations in New York and two in Los
    Angeles.

Websites

Because of the changing nature of Internet links,
Rosen Publishing has developed an online list of
websites related to the subject of this book. This site
is updated regularly. Please use this link to access
this list:

http://www.rosenlinks.com/COMEDY/Fallon

For Further Reading

Becker, Ron, Nick Marx, and Matt Sienkiewicz, eds. *Saturday Night Live and American TV.* Bloomington, IN: Indiana University Press, 2013.

Castle, Alison. *Saturday Night Live: The Book.* New York, NY: Taschen, 2015.

Dratch, Rachel. *Girl Walks into a Bar...Comedy Calamities, Dating Disasters, and a Midlife Miracle.* New York, NY: Gotham, 2012.

Fallon, Jimmy. *Thank You Notes.* New York, NY: Grand Central Publishing, 2011.

Fallon, Jimmy, and Gloria Fallon. *I Hate This Place: The Pessimist's Guide to Life.* New York, NY: Grand Central Publishing, 2003.

Gross, Terri. Interview with Jimmy Fallon on *Fresh Air*. National Public Radio broadcast May 23, 2011, posted on npr.com August 29, 2013. Retrieved May 31, 2015 (http://www.npr.org/2013/08/29/214910159/late-night-thank-you-notes-from-jimmy-fallon).

Hill, Doug. *Saturday Night: A Backstage History of Saturday Night Live*. Untreed Reads, 2014.

Hornby, Nick. *Fever Pitch.* New York, NY: Riverhead Books, 1998.

Kaplan, Steve. *The Hidden Tools of Comedy: The Serious Business of Being Funny.* Studio City, CA: Michael Weise Productions, 2013.

Leonard, Kelly, and Tom Yorton. *Yes, And: How Improvisation Reverses "No, But" Thinking and Improves Creativity and Collaboration—Lessons from The Second City.* New York, NY: HarperBusiness, 2015.

Libera, Ann. *The Second City Almanac of Improvisation.* Chicago, IL: Northwestern University Press, 2004.

Martin, Steve. *Born Standing Up: A Comic's Life.* New York, NY: Scribner, 2008.

Miller, James Andrew, and Tom Shales. *Live from New York: The Complete, Uncensored History of Saturday Night Live as Told by Its Stars, Writers, and Guests.* New York, NY: Little, Brown and Co., 2014.

Nichols, Sam. *Jimmy Fallon: Inside His Fight for Late Night on NBC.* Entertainment Legends E-Press, 2013.

Poehler, Amy. *Yes Please.* New York, NY: Dey Street Books, 2014.

Sacks, Mike. *Poking a Dead Frog: Conversations with Today's Top Comedy Writers.* New York, NY: Penguin, 2014.

Thompson, Amir "Questlove," and Ben Greenman. *Mo' Meta Blues: The World According to Questlove.* New York, NY: Grand Central Publishing, 2013.

Toplyn, Joe. *Comedy Writing for Late-Night TV: How to Write Monologue Jokes, Desk Pieces, Sketches, Parodies, Audience Pieces, Remotes, and Other Short-Form Comedy*. Rye, NY: Twenty Lane Media, 2014.

Tropiano, Stephen. *Saturday Night Live FAQ: Everything Left to Know About Television's Longest Running Comedy*. Milwaukee, WI: Applause Books, 2013.

Walsh, Matt, and Ian Roberts. *Upright Citizens Brigade Comedy Improvisation Manual.* New York, NY: Comedy Council of Nicea, 2013.

Bibliography

Blake, Meredith. "Jimmy Fallon: Critics Weigh in on 'Tonight Show' Debut." *Los Angeles Times*, February 18, 2014. Retrieved June 3, 2015 (http://www.latimes.com/entertainment/tv/showtracker/la-et-st-jimmy-fallon-tonight-show-debut-reviews-20140218-story.html).

Drew, April. "Irish Honor for Jimmy Fallon with Irish Spirit Award." IrishCentral.com, February 25, 2010. Retrieved May 30, 2015 (http://www.irishcentral.com/culture/entertainment/irish-honor-for-jimmy-fallon-with-irish-spirit-award-85354367-237686051.html).

Durbin, Jonathan. "A Man for All Reasons: Jimmy Fallon." *Paper*, November 1, 2001. Retrieved June 1, 2015 (http://www.papermag.com/2001/11/a_man_for_all_reasons_jimmy_fallon.php).

Fey, Tina. *Bossypants.* New York, NY: Little, Brown and Co., 2011.

Groundlings. "History." Retrieved May 31, 2015 (http://www.groundlings.com/history/beginning.aspx).

Hiatt, Brian. "Jimmy Fallon's Big Adventure." *Rolling Stone*, January 20, 2011. Retrieved May 31, 2015 (http://www.rollingstone.com/music/news/jimmy-fallons-big-adventure-20110120).

Hodge, Alison. *Twentieth Century Acting Training.* New York, NY: Routledge, 2001.

Itzkoff, David. "Extended Interview with Jimmy Fallon." *New York Times*, August 22, 2013.

Retrieved May 31, 2015 (http://www.nytimes. com/2013/08/25/arts/television/jimmy-fallon- snl-audition-interview.html?_r=0).

McGoldrick, Debbie. "'Night' Right for Jimmy Fallon." IrishCentral.com, March 14, 2009. Retrieved May 30, 2015 (http://www.irishcen- tral.com/culture/entertainment/late-nights -all-right-with-fallon-41094027-237630181. html).

Michell, Sia. "Fallon Comes Alive." *Spin*, March 2002, pp. 70–76.

NBC.com. "About *The Tonight Show Starring Jimmy Fallon.*" Retrieved May 31, 2015 (http://www. nbc.com/the-tonight-show/about).

O'Connell, Michael. "Four Months into Jimmy Fallon's 'Tonight,' *Late Night* Flourishes." *Hollywood Reporter*, June 5, 2014. Retrieved June 1, 2015 (http://www.hollywoodreporter. com/live-feed/four-months-jimmy-fallons -tonight-709605).

Paskin, Willa. "Jimmy Fallon Brings Earnest, Nice- Guy Vibe to His First *Tonight Show.*" *Slate*, February 18, 2014. Retrieved June 3, 2015 (http://www.slate.com/blogs/browbeat/ 2014/02/18/jimmy_fallon_s_first_tonight_show_ with_will_smith_and_u2_nice_earnest_pretty. html).

Rahman, Ray. "Entertainer of the Year." *Entertainment Weekly*, December 3, 2014.

Retrieved June 1, 2015 (http://www.ew.com/ ew/static/longform/ fallon/desktop/).

Rose, Tim. "Jimmy Fallon on Taking Over for Conan: 'I'm Putting Everything I Got Into This.'" Xfinity.com, February 23, 2009. Retrieved June 1, 2015 (http://my.xfinity.com/ blogs/tv/2009/02/23/jimmy-fallon-on-taking -over-for-conan-im-putting-everything-i- got-into-this).

Stanley, Alessandra. "Jimmy Fallon Debuts New *Tonight Show* in New York." *New York Times*, February 18, 2014. Retrieved June 3, 2015 (http://www.nytimes.com/2014/02/19/arts/ television/jimmy-fallon-debuts-new-tonight- show-in-new-york.html).

Sternbergh, Adam. "Mr. Sunshine." *New York*, November 7, 2010. Retrieved June 3, 2015 (http://nymag.com/arts/tv/profiles/69366).

Thompson, Amir, and Ben Greenman. "Questlove: Michell Bachmann Almost Got Me Fired from Jimmy Fallon Show." *Salon*, June 22, 2013. Retrieved May 31, 2015 (http://www.salon. com/2013/06/22/questlove_michele_ bachmann_almost_got_me_fired_from_jimmy_ fallon_show).

Timberlake, Justin. "The 2013 Time 100: Jimmy Fallon." *Time*, April 18, 2013. Retrieved May 31, 2015 (http://time100.time.com/2013/04/18/ time-100/slide/jimmy-fallon/).

Vanity Fair. "Jimmy Fallon: Lorne Michaels Advised Me on Who to Date (And Not Marry)." January 7, 2014. Retrieved May 30, 2015 (http://www.vanityfair.com/news/2014/01/jimmy-fallon-lorne-michaels-advised-me-on-who-to-date-and-not-marry).

Zafar, Aylin. "8 Times Questlove Is an Adorable, Awesome Music Nerd in His New Book." *Buzzfeed*, June 18, 2013. Retrieved May 31, 2015 (http://www.buzzfeed.com/azafar/8-times-questlove-is-an-adorable-awesome-music-nerd-in-his-n#.xwGwoB9KM).

Index

About the Author

Rebecca T. Klein holds a B.A. in English from Marygrove College in Detroit, Michigan, and an M.A. in English/Education from Brooklyn College. She has written several books for young adults and has worked with young people for many years as a camp counselor, camp director, and teacher. All of her work is driven by her commitment to social justice and anti-racism.

Photo Credits

Cover, p. 3 Helga Esteb/Shutterstock.com; cover background, interior pages (curtain) Kostsov/Shutterstock.com; pp. 6, 40-41, 54-55, 85 Theo Wargo/Getty Images; p. 12 Debra L Rothenberg/FilmMagic/Getty Images; pp. 14-15 NBC Television/Archive Photos/Getty Images; pp. 16-17 Dave Hogan/Hulton Archive/Getty Images; p. 25 Cindy Ord/Getty Images; p. 27 Joe Schilling/The LIFE Images Collection/Getty Images; pp. 28-29 Imeh Akpanudosen/Getty Images; pp. 36-37 KMazur/WireImage/Getty Images; p. 44 Kevin Mazur/WireImage/Getty Images; pp. 46-47 Jamie McCarthy/Getty Images; pp. 50-51 Jon Kopaloff/FilmMagic/Getty Images; pp. 58-59 Raleigh News & Observer/Tribune News Service/Getty Images; pp. 60-61 Jason Kempin/NBCUniversal/Getty Images; p. 66 Steve Mack/FilmMagic/Getty Images; pp. 68-69 Gilbert Carrasquillo/Getty Images; p. 75 Bloomberg/Getty Images; pp. 78-79 NBC/Photofest © NBC; p. 83 Kevin Winter/Getty Images.

Designer: Nicole Russo; Editor: Meredith Day; Photo Research: Bruce Donnola